BLS WORKING PAPERS

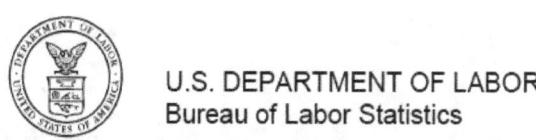 U.S. DEPARTMENT OF LABOR
Bureau of Labor Statistics

OFFICE OF PRICES AND LIVING
CONDITIONS

Constructing Household Specific Consumer Price Indexes:
An Analysis of Different Techniques and Methods

Robert A. Cage, U.S. Bureau of Labor Statistics
Thesia I. Garner, U.S. Bureau of Labor Statistics
Javier Ruiz-Castillo, Universidad Carlos III de Madrid

Working Paper 354
March 2002

Cage is an economist (email: Cage_R@BLS.GOV; telephone: (202) 691-6957) and Garner is a senior research economist (email: Garner_T@BLS.GOV; (202) 691-6579) with the Bureau of Labor Statistics. Ruiz-Castillo is a professor of economics (email: JRC@ECO.UC3M.ES; telephone: +34 1 624 95 88) at the Department of Economics, Universidad Carlos III de Madrid. All views expressed in this paper are those of the authors and do not reflect the views or policies of the Bureau of Labor Statistics or the Department of Economics, Universidad Carlos III de Madrid.

Constructing Household Specific Consumer Price Indexes:
An Analysis of Different Techniques and Methods

Robert A. Cage
Division of Consumer Prices and Price Indexes
and
Thesia I. Garner
Division of Price and Index Number Research
Bureau of Labor Statistics
Postal Square Building
2 Massachusetts Avenue N.E., Washington, D. C. 20212
UNITED STATES
and
Javier Ruiz-Castillo
Department of Economics
Universidad Carlos III de Madrid
Madrid 126, Getafe
Madrid 28903
SPAIN

July 6, 2001

Cage is an economist (email: Cage_R@BLS.GOV; telephone: (202) 606-6957) and Garner is a senior research economist (email: Garner_T@BLS.GOV; (202) 606-6579) with the Bureau of Labor Statistics. Ruiz-Castillo is a professor of economics (email: JRC@ECO.UC3M.ES; telephone: +34 1 624 95 88) at the Department of Economics, Universidad Carlos III de Madrid. All views expressed in this paper are those of the authors and do not reflect the views or policies of the Bureau of Labor Statistics or the Department of Economics, Universidad Carlos III de Madrid.

This research was begun in the summer of 1996 when Ruiz-Castillo was an ASA/NSF/BLS Research Fellow in the Office of Survey Methods Research at the Bureau of Labor Statistics and has been supported by the Bureau and by the Department of Economics, Universidad Carlos III de Madrid. An earlier version of this paper was presented at the 1997 National Bureau of Economic Research Summer Institute on Price Index Measurement. We thank Barbara Fraumeni for her comments as the discussant of the paper and others attending the summer institute for theirs as well. Special thanks are also extended to our colleagues in the Divisions of Consumer Prices and Price Indexes, and Price and Index Number Research for their comments and suggestions, especially Mary Kokoski, Brent Moulton and Patrick Jackman. Thanks are also extended to Anthony Yezer, George Washington University, for suggestions and discussions.

ABSTRACT

The primary purpose of this study is to produce household specific price indexes for consumer units or households living in the United States in the early 1990s. This paper is a report on how these household specific indexes were created. With household specific indexes, households are assumed to have nonhomothetic preferences, so changes in prices involve relative price changes between different sets of commodities and the resulting indexes will differ systematically between different households. We examine several different approaches to construct these indexes. Our indexes are based on internal U.S. Consumer Expenditure Survey (CEX) data for 1990-91 and Bureau of Labor Statistics Consumer Price Index (CPI) data from winter 1981, 1987, and 1991. Our base period is 1990-91. Using these data we produce Paasche type household specific indexes. In addition we propose an alternative definition of total expenditures, based on the CPI market basket commodity space, to be used for welfare analysis. Our underlying motivation for conducting this study was to compare real welfare inequality in Spain and the U.S. in the 1980s for another study (Garner et al. forthcoming 1997). Because of this comparison, we were somewhat restricted in our approach.

CEX data are used to calculate CPI market basket item budget shares for each interviewed household. Price indexes are merged with the household budget data at various levels of geographic and market basket item aggregation, and the variability in these indexes are compared in order to measure the value of using detailed consumption space over aggregated consumption space. In this study we introduce two novel approaches to producing household specific price indexes using BLS data. First, expenditure data from the Consumer Expenditure Diary survey, which is more detailed than the Interview, are used to impute missing consumption items for the Interview households. And second, a method to impute household indexes for the rural population is presented. Two different types of samples, horizontal and vertical (based on assumptions about the Interview households selected to define the base period), are used to provide the weights for the price indexes. Indexes are presented based on Interview only items and all items commodity spaces for the horizontal and vertical samples with additional indexes produced for consumer units living in urban and rural areas.

From our study we conclude that indexes based on expenditures for the horizontal and vertical samples do not differ significantly for the time periods of our study. However, differences in the indexes do result for the urban versus rural samples, with consumer units living in urban areas facing greater changes in relative prices than are faced by consumer units living in rural areas. The all-item indexes produced slightly higher index values than did the Interview-only item indexes. Relative prices appear to be pro-poor during the 1980s.

I. Introduction

Price changes affect households differently if households have varying patterns of expenditures, reflecting disparity in tastes and preferences. Most official measures of inflation, like the U.S. Consumer Price Index, are aggregate indexes which are based on data reflecting some representative or average household. However, different groups in the population are likely to have faster or slower growth in their real expenditures than is recorded by changes in the official CPI. Thus with nonhomothetic preferences, richer households will have larger budget shares for luxuries and smaller budget shares for necessities so that if changes in prices involve relative price changes between luxuries and necessities, the index will differ systematically between poor and rich households (Deaton and Muellbauer 1991). Because of this, it is desirable to use household specific price indexes to adjust expenditures when examining changes in real inequality over time.

In this paper, we examine several different approaches to constructing household specific consumer price indexes. U. S. Consumer Expenditure Survey (CEX) data from 1990-91 are used to calculate Consumer Price Index (CPI) market basket item budget shares for each interviewed consumer unit (also referred to as "household" in this study). In general a consumer unit is a collection of people who share a budget and some living quarters (see Appendix 1 for more details). Price indexes from 1981, 1987 and 1991 are merged with the household budget data at various levels of geographic and market basket item aggregation, and the variability in these indexes are compared

1

in order to measure the value of using detailed consumption space over aggregated consumption space.

We use as our base sample of consumer units those participating in the CEX Interview survey in 1990-91. We produce two sets of indexes for the commodity space bundles: one which is entirely based on CEX Interview data (141 items) and another which is based on a combination of Interview and Diary data (207 items). The difference between the Interview-only consumption bundle (hereafter referred to as X141) and the full consumption bundle (hereafter referred to as X207) reflects the fact that the Diary collects more detailed expenditure information than does the Interview. The use of the Diary data to impute and allocate more specific commodities to the Interview sample is novel and has not been used in previous studies (as far as we know). Another novel approach followed in this study is to create household indexes for the rural population based on the relative prices faced by urban nonmetropolitan consumer units living in various geographic areas.[1] Thus, price indexes are produced for urban and rural consumer units as well as for the combined sample. We also produce indexes for samples based on two different sample structures which we refer to as horizontal and vertical. For the vertical sample, a quarterly Interview is treated as an independent and separate case (there are a maximum of four Interviews per consumer

---

[1] The official CPI-U represents about 84 percent of the total U.S. noninstitutional population. The rural sector of the country is not included in the population universe of the CPI-U. Monthly price relatives are not available for rural areas. In order to include the rural portion of the CEX Interview sample in our study, we assigned the available price indexes for the urban nonmetropolitan areas (or "D-sized" areas) to rural households by geographic region (Northeast, Midwest, South, and West).

unit). In the horizontal sample, expenditures from every interview available for the consumer unit are aggregated together.

Inflation experience between 'the winter of 1981 and the winter 1991' and 'the winter of 1987 and the winter of 1991' are measured for each consumer unit. Since current period weights (winter 1991) are used to produce the indexes, Paasche indexes result. The base period is winter (January, February, and March) 1991. This period was selected as the base in order to match our indexes with those produced for a joint Spanish-U.S. comparison of expenditure inequality (Garner et al., forthcoming 1997).

Our study is different from others (e.g, Jorgenson and Slesnick (1983), and Kokoski (1987)) who have produced household specific price indexes for consumer units living in the U.S. First, we use a broader commodity space than has been used in the past to produce the indexes. Second, we impute price indexes to consumer units living in rural areas. Third, we use more recent data than have been used in the past. And fourth, we test the sensitivity of our results to assumptions made about the base sample upon which the indexes are based: whether the indexes differ when quarterly expenditures are assumed to be independent or not. The base samples are referred to as horizontal and vertical; quarterly independence is assumed for the vertical sample but not for the horizontal sample.

From our study we conclude that indexes based on expenditures for the horizontal and vertical samples do not differ significantly for the time periods under investigation. However, differences in the indexes do result for the urban versus rural samples, with consumer units living in urban areas facing greater changes in relative prices than are faced by consumer units living in rural areas. The X207 or all items indexes produce slightly higher index values than did the X141 or Interview only item indexes. Relative prices appear to be pro-poor during the 1980's. All analyses are based on unweighted data.

The remainder of the paper is divided into four sections. In section two, we present our motivation for this study. In section three we describe the data and index number construction methods that we used. Section four includes our results, while section five provides a summary and conclusion.

II. Motivation

It has long been recognized in the empirical literature that different groups are not affected in the same manner by the evaluation of relative prices (for early studies on India, see Iyengar (1967) and Mahalanobis (1972); for U.K. studies, see Prais (1959), Nicholson (1975), Lesser (1976), and the references quoted in Muellbauer (1974b); for the U.S., see Amble and Stewart (1994), Garner et al. (1996), Michael (1970), Hollister and Palmer (1972), Hagemann (1982), Jorgenson and Slesnick (1983), Kokoski (1987), and Snyder (1961); and for Spain, see Abadia (1986)). However, it appears that the idea that price movements should be included in intertemporal income inequality comparisons was originally suggested by Iyengar and Battacharya (1965), some time before the path-breaking work of Atkinson (1970), Kolm (1976a, b), and Sen (1973) on the axiomatic foundations of inequality measurement. Subsequently, Muellbauer (1974a) proved that an inequality measure derived from a strictly quasi-concave social welfare function, defined over the distribution of individual indirect utility levels, is independent of price changes if and only if preferences are identical and homothetic for all consuming units. We do not accept such strong restrictions on individual preferences, thus our choice to use household specific price indexes for our comparison of real inequality.

In the absence of such strong restrictions on individual preferences, the usual procedure of expressing two income distributions at common prices by using a single inflation rate for all individuals is not warranted. The reason, of course, is that changes in relative prices have redistributive consequences. Therefore, changes in money inequality need not coincide with changes in real inequality.

To estimate the change in real inequality we need household specific price indexes. But once armed with a set of such price indexes, we may use them for other interesting purposes, like the estimation of the real change in poverty or welfare, or the construction of group price indexes for relevant partitions of the population.

There are two approaches to construct household specific price indexes. For one, a complete commodity demand system could be estimated, which in turn would be used to construct a true cost of living index for every household (Muellbauer 1974a, 1974b, Slesnick). Second, one could construct a set of household specific statistical price indexes. All that is neded for this second approach is a vector of price relatives at the maximum disaggregation level, provided by the statistical agency in charge of the official consumer price index, and a vector of household specific budget shares defined on the corresponding commodity space. It is well known that at the individual level, statistical price indexes of the Laspeyres (Paasche) type provide an upper (lower) bound for the corresponding theoretical constructions (See, for example, Pollak, Diewert). Consequently, in this approach we can only hope to estimate convenient bounds for the change in real terms of the social concepts of interest, namely, the change in the mean, poverty, inequality, or welfare.

Recently, the second approach has been applied in Spain on the basis of three large household budget surveys, the Encuestas de Presupuestos Familiares (or EPF for short), collected by the Spanish Instituto Nacional de Estadística (INE for short) with the main purpose of estimating the weights of the official consumer price index.[2]

Coming now to the evidence during the 80's in the U.S., most of the literature points to an increase in earnings, income and consumption inequality, however measured. In particular, using CEX data at the BLS, Johnson and Shipp (1996) find that "consumption inequality peaks in 1986 and then falls slightly, peaks again in 1990 and 1991 and falls during 1993 and 1994." In their conclusions, these authors suggest that "...using Slottje (1987) and Slesnick (1994) as a starting point, the next stage of research [should] examine how inflation and prices affect inequality."

Given the tightness of the empirical bounds obtained in the Spanish case for the relevant conceptual constructs, we have started a program to study the following two

---

[2] Higueras and Ruiz-Castillo (1992) construct household specific price indexes using the EPFs of 1973-74 and 1980-81. Ruiz-Castillo (1995, 1997) compares the changes in real inequality and welfare from 1973-74 to 1980-81. Ruiz-Castillo and Sastre (1996) construct household specific price indexes for the 1990-91 EPF. Del Río and Ruiz-Castilllo (1996, 1997a, 1997b, 1997c) compare real inequality and poverty from 1980-81 to 1990-91. Sastre (1997) compares in real terms the three available EPFs.

topics: (1) the evolution of household expenditures real inequality in the U.S. during the 80´s, using household specific statistical price indexes to capture the distributional role of changes in relative prices; and (2) the comparison of household expenditure inequality and welfare between the U.S. and Spain.

In the Spanish studies, the 1990-91 household expenditure distribution at current prices is expressed at constant prices of the 1991 winter (by means of Laspeyres price indexes) and the 1981 winter (by means of Paasche price indexes). Correspondingly, in this paper we use CEX data to construct several alternatives for the U.S. distribution of household expenditures at current prices for the 1990-91 reference period. Then we construct Laspeyres and Paasche household specific statistical price indexes to express these distributions at winter 1991 and winter 1981 constant prices.

In addition, to test the Johnson and Shipp (1996) finding of a change in the trend in inequality during the mid 80´s, we express also the 1990-91 household expenditures distributions at winter 1987 constant prices. Applying the lessons learned in this paper, in order to study the change in real household expenditures inequality and welfare during the 80's we plan to extract from CEX data a 1980-81 household expenditures distribution, and to construct household specific price indexes to express it at winter 1981, winter 1987 and winter 1991 constant prices.

III. Construction of Household Specific Price Indexes

To evaluate the options we take in regard to these points, it is important to understand how the official aggregate consumer price index is constructed. In both Spain and the U.S., the CPI (Consumer Price Index) is a fixed weight price index calculated according to a modified Laspeyres formula. In both countries the fixed weights are estimated from the microeconomic information provided by a household budget survey. There are two main differences. First, the Spanish EPF is a representative sample of consumer units interviewed during a given year, while the CEX is a continuous budget survey in which one fourth of of all households rotate every quarter and every household provide expenditure data during four consecutive quarters. Second, the EPF is a single instrument for the collection of expenditures on all types of goods and services, while the CEX consists of two separate instruments: a Diary during a period of two weeks, focused on the recording of expenditures on items with a high frequency of purchase, and an Interview which records all expenditures during a three month period.

To place in context our treatment of the U.S. case, we start this section with a brief review of the much simpler Spanish case.

A. The Spanish Case

In the Spanish case, the EPF is a household budget survey in which interviews are spread out uniformly over a period of 52 weeks. All household members 14 years of age or older are supposed to record all expenditures taking place during a sample week. Then, in-depth interviews are conducted to register past expenditures over reference periods beyond a week and up to a year. From that information the INE estimates annual household total expenditures. For the details on the last two EPFs, collected from April 1980 to March 1981 and from April 1990 to March 1991, respectively, see INE (1983) and INE (1992).

Let there be H and H' households in the two situations, and let $\mathbf{x} = (x^1,..., x^H)$ and $\mathbf{y} = (y^1,..., y^{H'})$ be the 1980-81 and 1990-91 distributions of household expenditures, respectively. Let j = 1,...J denote the subset of items for which the INE constructs the Spanish *Indice de Precios de Consumo* (or IPC for short). For each h, we can write $x^h = \Sigma_j$

$x_{h;j}$, where $x_{h;j}$ is household h expenditure on commodity j. Let X_j be the aggregate expenditure on commodity j, i.e., $X_j = \Sigma_h x_{h;j}$, and let X be the aggregate expenditure on all commodities, i.e., $X = \Sigma_j X_j = \Sigma_j \Sigma_h x_{h;j}$. The fixed weights for the official IPC are given by the J-dimensional vector $\mathbf{W} = (W_1,..., W_J)$, where $W_j = X_j /X$. The IPC for period t, based in the period 1983, is then computed according to the modified Laspeyres formula

$$IPC_{t,0} = ML(\mathbf{p}_t, \mathbf{p}_0; \mathbf{W}) = \Sigma_j W_j (p_{tj}/p_{0j}),$$

where $\mathbf{p}_t$ = price vector in period t, and $\mathbf{p}_0$ = price vector in the base year 1983[Note *].

It is well known that the overall IPC is a weighted average of the household specific IPC's. Let $\mathbf{w}^h = (w_{h;1},..., w_{h;J})$ be household h vector of budget shares, with $w_{h;j} = x_{h;j}/x^h$. The modified Laspeyres IPC for household h is given by

$$IPC_0^{h;t} = ML(\mathbf{p}_t, \mathbf{p}_0; \mathbf{w}^h) = \Sigma_j w_{h;j} (p_{tj}/p_{0j}).$$

Let $\alpha^h = x^h /X$, so that $\Sigma_h \alpha^h = 1$. It is easy to see that, for each j,

$$W_j = \Sigma_h \alpha^h w_j.$$

Therefore,

$$IPC_{t,0} = \Sigma_h \alpha^h IPC_0^{h;t}.$$

In other words, the overall IPC is equal to the weighted average of the individual IPC's with weights equal to household expenditures. This is the reason why the IPC is called a "plutocratic" price index in which the rich weight more than the poor[Note **].

Which is the connection between this individual IPC and the corresponding true cost-of-living index? It is often forgotten that the answer is: none. To understand this point, let us assume that household h has a utility function U^h defined on the J-dimensional vector of quantities $\mathbf{q}^h = (q_{h;1},..., q_{h;J})$. Let us divide the Spanish collection

9

period into four quarters indexed by s = 1,..., 4, where 1 = Spring 1980, 2 = Summer 1980, 3 = Fall 1980, and 4 = Winter 1981, and assign each household to the quarter in which it is interviewed. We *assume* that a household h interviewed in quarter s with annual total expenditures $x_{h;s}$ faces a vector of current prices $\mathbf{p}_s = (p_{s1},..., p_{sJ})$. Denote by $\mathbf{q}_{h;s} = (q_{h;s1},..., q_{h;sJ})$ the solution to household h's utility maximization problem restricted to $\Sigma_j p_{sj} q_{h;sj} \leq x_{h;s}$. If we denote by φ^h the indirect utility function and by c^h the expenditure or cost function, we have that $u_{h;s} = \varphi^h(x_{h;s}, \mathbf{p}_s)$ and $x_{h;s} = \mathbf{p}_s \mathbf{q}_{h;s} = c^h(u_{h;s}, \mathbf{p}_s)$. Then the cost-of-living index to compare price vectors $\mathbf{p}_t$ and $\mathbf{p}_0$ maintaining constant the utility level $u_{h;s}$ is defined by

$$CL(\mathbf{p}_t, \mathbf{p}_0; u_{h;s}) = c^h(u_{h;s}, \mathbf{p}_t)/c^h(u_{h;s}, \mathbf{p}_0).$$

Clearly, between $IPC_0^{h;t}$ and $CL(\mathbf{p}_t, \mathbf{p}_0; u_{h;s})$ there need not be any connection at all.

This negative result does not preclude an appropriate solution to the comparison of the money distributions $\mathbf{x} = (x^1,..., x^H)$ and $\mathbf{y} = (y^1,..., y^{H'})$ at constant prices. We first choose the winter of 1991 as the period in which to express both distributions. For this purpose, we begin by computing a set of Laspeyres statistical price indices for the 1980-81 households. For each household h interviewed in quarter s = 1,..., 4, we have

$$L(\mathbf{p}_t, \mathbf{p}_s; w_{h;s}) = \Sigma_j w_{h;sj} (p_{tj}/p_{sj}) = \mathbf{p}_t \mathbf{q}_{h;s}/\mathbf{p}_s \mathbf{q}_{h;s},$$
where
$$(p_{tj}/p_{sj}) = (p_{tj}/p_{0j})/(p_{sj}/p_{0j})$$

t = winter 1991, and 0 = 1983. Consider the Laspeyres cost-of-living index $CL(\mathbf{p}_t, \mathbf{p}_s; u_{h;s})$ to compare price vectors $\mathbf{p}_t$ and $\mathbf{p}_s$ mantaining constant the utility level $u_{h;s}$:
$$CL(\mathbf{p}_t, \mathbf{p}_s; u_{h;s}) = c^h(u_{h;s}, \mathbf{p}_t)/c^h(u_{h;s}, \mathbf{p}_s) = c^h(u_{h;s}, \mathbf{p}_t)/\mathbf{p}_s \mathbf{q}_{h;s}.$$

Now, clearly we have:

$$CL(\mathbf{p}_{t'}, \mathbf{p}_s; u_{h;s}) \leq L(\mathbf{p}_{t'}, \mathbf{p}_s; w_{h;s}).$$

That is, the household specific Laspeyres statistical price index, $L(\mathbf{p}_{t'}, \mathbf{p}_s; w_{h;s})$, is an upper bound of the corresponding Laspeyres cost-of-living index $CL(\mathbf{p}_{t'}, \mathbf{p}_s; u_{h;s})$. Denote by $x_{h;t}$ household expenditures $x_{h;s}$ at prices $\mathbf{p}_t$. Ideally we would like to estimate $x_{h;t}$ by the product $x_{h;s}$ times $CL(\mathbf{p}_{t'}, \mathbf{p}_s; u_{h;s})$. However, in the absence of a knowledge of household preferences, we must be content to estimate that magnitude as $x_{h;t} = x_{h;s} L(\mathbf{p}_{t'}, \mathbf{p}_s; w_{h;s}) = \mathbf{p}_t \, q_{h;s}$, which provides an upper bound to the true construct.

For the 1990-91 distribution, let $\mathbf{v}_{h;sj'} = (v_{h;s1},..., v_{h;sJ})$ be the vector of budget shares of household h interviewed in quarter s of the 1990-91 EPF, where $v_{h;sj} = y_{h;j}/y^h$ and $s = 1,..., 4$ with $1 =$ Spring 1990, $2 =$ Summer 1990, $3 =$ Fall 1990, and $4 =$ Winter 1991, Then, for every h and s we can estimate

$$L(\mathbf{p}_{t'}, \mathbf{p}_s; v_{h;s}) = \Sigma_j \, v_{h;sj} \, (p_{tj}/p_{sj}) = \mathbf{p}_t \, q_{h;s}/\mathbf{p}_s \, q_{h;s}.$$

Similarly, $y_{h;t} = y_{h;s} L(\mathbf{p}_{t'}, \mathbf{p}_s; v_{h;s}) = \mathbf{p}_t \, q_{h;s}$ provides also an upper bound to the true construct. Distributions $\mathbf{x}_t = (x_{1;t},..., x_{H;t})$ and $\mathbf{y}_t = (y_{1;t},..., y_{H';t})$ are both expressed at constant winter 1991 prices, and can be compared for the purpose of inequality, poverty and welfare in real terms.

Since we are interested in expressing both money distributions at prices of situation 1, we now choose $t' =$ winter of 1981. We construct statistical Laspeyres price indices $L(\mathbf{p}_{t''}, \mathbf{p}_s; w_{h;s})$ for the 1980-81 household distribution, and Paasche price indices $P(\mathbf{p}_{t''}, \mathbf{p}_s; v_{h;s})$ for the 1990-91 household distribution:

$$L(\mathbf{p}_{t''}, \mathbf{p}_s; w_{h;s}) = \Sigma_j \, w_{h;sj} \, (p_{t'j}/p_{sj}) = \mathbf{p}_{t'} \, q_{h;s}/\mathbf{p}_s \, q_{h;s'}$$

$$P(\mathbf{p}_{t''}, \mathbf{p}_s; v_{h;s}) = 1/(\Sigma_j \, v_{h;sj} \, (p_{t'j}/p_{sj})) = \mathbf{p}_s \, q_{h;s}/\mathbf{p}_{t'} \, q_{h;s'}$$

where

$$(p_{tj}/p_{sj}) = (p_{tj}/p_{0j})/(p_{sj}/p_{0j}),$$

t' = winter 1981, 0 = 1983, and s = 1,..., 4 with 1 = Spring 1980 or 1990, 2 = Summer 1980 or 1990, 3 = Fall 1980 or 1990, and 4 = Winter 1981 or 1991. Now we can compare in real terms $\mathbf{x}_{t'} = (x_{1;t'},..., x_{H;t'})$ and $\mathbf{y}_{t'} = (y_{1;t'},..., y_{H';t'})$, where $x_{h;t'} = x_{h;s} L(\mathbf{p}_{t'}, \mathbf{p}_s; \mathbf{w}_{h;s})$ and $y_{h;t'} = y_{h;s}/P(\mathbf{p}_{t'}, \mathbf{p}_s; \mathbf{v}_{h;s})$. Since statistical Paasche price indices provide a lower bound for the corresponding Paasche cost-of-living indices, for every h our estimate $y_{h;t'}$ is an upper bound for the true construct.

Finally, we can consider the rate of inflation from period t' to period t measured according to 1980-81 and 1990-91 household tastes. First, for each h interviewed in quarter s of 1980-81, we can define a cost-of-living index

$$CL(\mathbf{p}_t, \mathbf{p}_{t'}; \mathbf{u}_{h;s}) = c^h(u_{h;s}, \mathbf{p}_t)/c^h(u_{h;s}, \mathbf{p}_{t'}).$$

Notice that $x_{h;t} = \mathbf{p}_t \mathbf{q}_{h;s}$ and $x_{h;t'} = \mathbf{p}_{t'} \mathbf{q}_{h;s}$ provide an upper bound for $c^h(u_{h;s}, \mathbf{p}_t)$ and $c^h(u_{h;s}, \mathbf{p}_{t'})$, respectively. Since period t = winter 1991 is further apart from 1980-81 than period t' = winter 1981, we expect that the rate of inflation approximated by

$$x_{h;t}/x_{h;t'} = \mathbf{p}_t \mathbf{q}_{h;s}/\mathbf{p}_{t'} \mathbf{q}_{h;s}$$

provides an upper bound for the true construct $CL(\mathbf{p}_t, \mathbf{p}_{t'}; \mathbf{u}_{h;s})$. Second, for each h interviewed in quarter s of 1990-91, we can similarly define a cost-of-living index $CL(\mathbf{p}_t, \mathbf{p}_{t'}; \mathbf{u}_{h;s})$ which can be approximated by

$$y_{h;t}/y_{h;t'} = \mathbf{p}_t \mathbf{q}_{h;s}/\mathbf{p}_{t'} \mathbf{q}_{h;s}.$$

Now we expect that $y_{h;t'}$ provides a worse upper bound approximation to $\mathbf{p}_{t'} \mathbf{q}_{h;s}$ than $y_{h;t}$ relative to $\mathbf{p}_t \mathbf{q}_{h;s}$. Therefore, our estimate of the rate of inflation from period t' to period t, measured according to 1990-91 household tastes, provides a lower bound to

12

the true construct $CL(\mathbf{p}_{t'}, \mathbf{p}_{t'}; \mathbf{u}_{h;s})$. Of course, there is no *a priori* reason to expect the distribution of $CL(\mathbf{p}_{t'}, \mathbf{p}_{t'}; \mathbf{u}_{h;s})$ for the 1980-81 households to be, on average, greater or smaller than the distribution of $CL(\mathbf{p}_{t'}, \mathbf{p}_{t'}; \mathbf{u}_{h;s})$ for the 1990-91 households. However, in practice we would prefer to find that our lower bound estimate according to 1990-91 tastes is below our upper bound estimate according to 1980-81 tastes.

B. The determination of the 1990-91 household expenditures distribution

The continuous and rotating nature of the CEX in the US case, poses special problems for the determination of the 1990-91 household expenditures distribution at current prices, that is, the equivalent of the **y** distribution in the Spanish case. In this subsection, we limit ourselves to the Interview survey only (See Appendix 1). Households are interviewed from one to five times, with the first interview used for bounding purposes only. Expenditures recorded in quarters 2 to 5 refer to those made in the previous three months. In the US case there are two ways to estimate annual expenditures y^h. On the one hand, we may assume that the quarters are independent so that each quarterly expenditure would be multiplied by four to obtain an annual value. On the other hand, we may recognize that quarters are not independent, in which case expenditures are the sum of four quarterly values recorded during the quarters in which the consumer unit participates in the survey. In the first case we have what we call a vertical sample, while in the second case we have a horizontal sample.

Let us begin with the horizontal sample. CEX files consist of all households who have provided one, two, three or four quarters of data. Restricting ourselves to so-called complete households with four quarters of data would be unnecessarily restrictive. Including some incomplete households allows us to increase the sample size. The obvious thing to do is to impute missing information with the help of the information actually recorded. Specifically, missing data are made equal to the average of non missing quarterly values. However, we do not think that it makes much sense imputing as many as three quarters of data. Therefore, we restrict ourselves to all households with at least two quarters of data.

In the horizontal case, the annual household expenditures is:

$$y^h = \Sigma_r \, y_{h;r}$$

where $y_{h;r}$ is household h's total expenditures -recorded or imputed- for quarter r. The sum goes over four quarters of data for each household selected. Which households should be included? Consider all households whose expenditures refer to the 1990-91 period, that is, those households whose second to fifth interviews are collected from the Summer 1990 (Q903) to the Spring 1991 (Q912). We say that these households belong to "Group 0". There are only 1,367 households in Group 0 with at least two quarters of data, a relatively small sample. We suggest to include also the following groups:

- Households for whom three quarters of data belong to the 1990-91 period, that is, households whose second to fifth interviews are collected from the spring 1990 (Q902) to the winter 1991 (Q911) [Group -1] and from the Fall 1990 (Q904) to the Summer 1991 (Q913) [Group +1].

-Households for whom two quarters of data belong to the 1990-91 period, that is, households whose second to fifth interviews are collected from the winter 1990 (Q901) to the fall 1990 (Q904) [Group -2] and from the winter 1991 (Q914) to the fall 1991 (Q914) [Group +2].

For these four additional groups, we require that the minimum two quarters of recorded data must fall inside the 1990-91 period. There are 4,917 households from these four groups. Therefore, the horizontal sample consists of 6,284 consumer units.

Table 1 provides an illustration of the horizontal sample design. "Quarter #" refers to the number of quarters from which we drew the Interview data; eight interview periods were used. "Collection quarter" refers to the quarter in which the data were collected (quarter one 1990 through quarter four 1991), while "expenditure reference quarter" refers to the reference period (quarter four 1989 through quarter three 1991) of the reported expenditures. The interview households eligible for the horizontal sample belong to the Groups -2 to +2 shaded in Table 1.

Table 1. Illustration of Horizontal and Vertical Sample Design

	Quarter #		1	2	3	4	5	6	7	8	
	Collection Quarter	Q894	Q901	Q902	Q903	Q904	**Q911**	Q912	Q913	Q914	Q921
	Expenditure Reference Quarter	Q893	Q894	Q901	Q902	Q903	**Q904**	Q911	Q912	Q913	Q914
	-3	2	3	4	5						
G	-2		2	3	4	5					
R	-1			2	3	4	5				
O	0				2	3	4	5			
U	1					2	3	4	5		
P	2						2	3	4	5	
	3							2	3	4	5

▨ Horizontal sample, quarterly interviews summed

☐ Vertical sample, quarterly interviews independent

In the vertical sample, the annual household expenditure is:

$$y^h = 4\, y_{h;s}$$

where $y_{h;s}$ is the quarterly data, and s = Spring 90,....,Winter 1991 as in the Spanish subsection. Which households should be included? To begin with, those households from Groups -2 through +2 satisfying two conditions: having at least two quarters of recorded expenditure data, and having one of them in the 1990-91 period. As we can see in Table 1, under these conditions we draw data from four different Groups with expenditures recorded in the two central quarters (Summer and Fall 1990), but at most

15

from three different Groups for the remaining quarters (Spring 1990, Winter 1991). Therefore, to have a balanced vertical sample, provided they have two quarters of data we include also those households with the fifth interview in Spring 1990 -Group -3- and those households with their second interview in Winter 1991 -Group +3. These are also indicated in Table 1.

C. Vector of budget shares

In order to define the vector of budget shares, we first need to define the commodity space. For Spain, a single survey instrument is used to collect expenditure data from a sample of consumer units considered to be representative of the total Spanish population and all commodities are covered in each interview. In contrast, two independent samples are used to collect data in the U.S. Using only data from the CEX Interview, 141 items (based on selected detailed expenditures and three global questions) are covered, while if we use the official CPI market basket structure, 207 items (based on a combination of Interview data and detailed expenditure reports available from the Diary and) are included.

The first step in the construction of budget shares for each household in both the vertical and horizontal sample was to map their reported expenditures to the 207 CPI market basket strata. Roughly 60 percent of the market basket (122 items) are defined in their entirety by expenditures reported in the CEX Interview. An additional 16 items are defined in part by the domain of the CEX Interview. Furthermore, aggregate estimates (based on global questions) are also available for food at home, food away from home, and alcohol at home. Thus, expenditure reports available for each household were partitioned into 141 items (3 at an aggregate level). See Appendix 2 for a listing of the item strata by source.

The remaining 68 items, consisting primarily of food, housekeeping supplies, and personal care expenditures, are available only from the CEX Diary. In order to

16

estimate expenditures at this level of detail for each household in the vertical and horizontal samples, CEX Diary data from 1990 and 1991 were used to allocate major expenses reported in the Interview to the item strata level. First, the average budget share of total food-at-home was calculated for each of the 52 food-at-home items, by index-area and consumer unit size in the Diary sample. These shares were then mapped to the CEX Interview sample by index-area and consumer unit size, and used to allocate the total food-at-home expenditure reported in the Interview to the detailed item. Similar allocations were performed for food-away-from home, alcohol at home, and the remaining Diary-specific items. This process also functioned to impute expenditures for roughly 40 specific goods and services not covered by the domain of the Interview (e.g., soaps, laundry and cleaning products, tolls, over-the-counter drugs, pet food, and personal care products). This was accomplished by calculating the expenditure for the Diary-unique item, as a percent of total food expense, and taking the product of this factor and the total food expense reported in the Interview.

Some expenditures were adjusted to meet CPI market basket definitions. These include (1) adjusting maintenance and repair goods and services and major appliance purchases made by homeowners to a ìrental equivalenceî definition; (2) adjusting homeowner insurance to reflect the portion covering personal property and to exclude the portion covering real property; (3) adjusting the expenditures for new vehicles to reflect gross purchase price and adjusting the expenditures for used vehicles to reflect ìdealer profitî; (4) adjusting the expenditures for health insurance to reflect ìretained earningsî and reallocating the remainder to other health care goods and services; (5) and other miscellaneous allocations. These adjustments were made using official CPI methodologies for consumer units included in the CPI-U (urban) population. The adjustments for rural consumer units were accomplished by using national averages to simulate the official methodologies (BLS 1997).

17

Ultimately, both in the vertical and the horizontal sample, two separate estimates of total CPI market basket expenditures were calculated for each household: one based on 141 items and one based on all 207 items. Recall that annual household expenditures in the vertical sample was defined as

$$y^h = 4\, y_{h;s},$$

where $y_{h;s}$ is the quarterly data, and s = Spring 90,...,Winter 1991. In the horizontal sample, annual household expenditures was estimated as

$$y^h = S_r\, y_{h;r},$$

where $y_{h;r}$ is household h's total expenditures -recorded or imputed- for quarter r. In both cases, denote the household h's budget shares vector by $v^h = (v_{h;1},...,v_{h;J})$, where J = 141, 207. Naturally, budget shares are defined differently for both samples. For a household h in quarter s of the vertical sample, we have:

$$v_{h;sj} = y_{h;sj}/y_{h;s}.$$

For a household h in the horizontal sample, we compute four sets of (quarterly) weights, one for each of the r quarters making up the annual household expenditures. The details are different for each Group (see Table 1):

$v_{h;rj} = y_{h;rj}/y_{h;r}$, with:

r = Fall 1989,..., Summer 1990 if h belongs to Group -2

r = Winter 1990,..., Fall1990 if h belongs to Group -1

r = Spring 1990,..., Winter 1991 if h belongs to Group 0

r = Summer 1990,..., Spring 1991 if h belongs to Group +1

r = Fall 1990,..., Summer 1991 if h belongs to Group +2.

D. Quarterly Item-Area Price Relatives

Monthly price indexes, p_{tj}/p_{0j}, based in period 0 = 1982-84, were first extracted for each item stratum-index area (item-area) combination for all months belonging to the quarters involved beyond the base period 1982-84, that is, Winter 1987 and from Fall 1989 through Summer 1991. An item-area cell represents the elementary level of aggregation in the CPI; that is, the lowest level at which price quotes are pooled together to estimate monthly price change. There are 41 areas and 207 items. In addition, aggregate monthly indexes for (a) food at home, (b) food away from home, and (c) alcohol at home were extracted for use in processing Interview-only consumption (see Appendix 2 for a listing of the item strata, and Table 3 for a listing of the index areas).

Obtaining price indexes for the 207 by 41 item-area matrix for the winter 81 months was more problematic. The item-area structure of the CPI at this time was based on the 1978 Revision market basket definition and does not represent a one-to-one correspondence with the 1987 Revision-based structure. A concordance between the 1978-structure and the 1987-structure was necessary to adjust the January 1987 price index $P_{i,a}^{t=8701}$ for each item-area to the winter 81 months. This was accomplished in two steps. First, $P_{i,a}^{t=8701}$ was adjusted to $P_{i,a}^{t=8301}$ using the concordance methodology first developed by Aizcorbe and Jackman (1993). Of note, sampling areas that did not exist prior to 1987 (i.e., Denver, New Orleans, and Tampa Bay) were moved by their corresponding region-city size area index pre-1987 (i.e., west-medium MSA, south-

19

medium MSA, and south-medium MSA, respectively). The January 1983 index for each item-area was calculated as:

(1)
$$P_{i,a}^{t=8301} = P_{i,a}^{t=8701} * \frac{P_{I,A}^{t=8301}}{P_{I,A}^{t=8701}}$$

where i = item stratum, 1987 structure; a = index area, 1987 structure; I = Aizcorbe/Jackman item concordance; A = Aizcorbe/Jackman area concordance. This imputation works for roughly 90 percent of the item-area cells. If no corresponding item-area cell existed in Aizcorbe/Jackman, then $P_{i,a}^{t=8301}$ was imputed by the average price relative for its expenditure class $\frac{P_{EC,A}^{t=8301}}{P_{EC,A}^{t=8701}}$.[3] This occurred for roughly 40 items. If there was no corresponding expenditure class, then $P_{i,a}^{t=8301}$ was imputed by the average price relative $\frac{P_{MG,A}^{t=8301}}{P_{MG,A}^{t=8701}}$ for its major group.[4] This method was used for maintenance and repair items, major appliances, and personal computers - items that were omitted from the Aizcorbe/Jackman research.

The second step in the estimation of $P_{i,a}^{t=81m}\big|_{m=1to3}$ was to deflate $P_{i,a}^{t=8301}$ by the price relative $\frac{P_{i,a}^{t=81m}\big|_{m=1to3}}{P_{i,a}^{t=8301}}$. Since item-area indexes prior to December 1982 could be obtained in neither a cost-effective nor timely manner, aggregate indexes at the region-

---

[3] An expenditure class is a grouping of item strata which are expected to have similar price movement. It is used to impute price change when actual price change data are not available.
[4] Major group for the purpose of this imputation was defined as food, housing, and all other items.

major expenditure group level were used.[5] The January, February, and March 1981 index for each item-area was calculated as:

$$(2) \qquad P_{i,a}^{t=81m}\Big|_{m=1to3} = P_{i,a}^{t=8301} * \frac{P_{MG,R}^{t=81m}}{P_{MG,R}^{t=8301}}$$

Finally, the arithmetic mean of the monthly indexes was calculated to represent the quarterly price index for each quarter in the study period:

$$(3) \qquad P_{i,a}^{q} = \frac{\sum_{t \in q; i,a} P_{i,a}^{t}}{3}$$

Long-term price relatives were then calculated by dividing each quarterly index by the index value in each of the expenditure reference quarters included in the study, (b=Q894 through Q913):

$$(4) \qquad P_{(q,b;i,a)} = \frac{P_{i,a}^{q}}{P_{i,a}^{b}}$$

All quarterly price relatives p_{tj}/p_{0j} were calculated as the simple average of the corresponding monthly data.

E. Household specific price indexes

We begin with urban households, the only ones for whom we have price relatives. Among them, let us start with the vertical sample. We want to express each

---

[5] Region defined as northeast, midwest, south, and east. Major expenditure class defined as (1) food and beverages, (2) utilities, (3) housefurnishings and services, (4) apparel, (5) transportation, (6) health care, (7) entertainment, (8) shelter, and (9) all other goods and services.

household annual expendituures at prices of winter 1981, 1987 and 1991. Let $(p_{tj}/p_{sj}) = (p_{tj}/p_{0j})/(p_{sj}/p_{0j})$. In the case of t = winter 1991, for each household h in quarter s = Spring 1990,..., Fall 1990 we construct the following Laspeyres indices:

$$L(\mathbf{p}_t, \mathbf{p}_s; \mathbf{v}_{h;s}) = S_j\, v_{h;sj}\, (p_{tj}/p_{sj}) = \mathbf{p}_t\, \mathbf{q}_{h;s}/\mathbf{p}_s\, \mathbf{q}_{h;s}.$$

When t = winter 1987, winter 1981, we need Paasche indices:

$$P(\mathbf{p}_t, \mathbf{p}_s; \mathbf{v}_{h;s}) = 1/(S_j\, v_{h;sj}\, (p_{tj}/p_{sj})) = \mathbf{p}_s\, \mathbf{q}_{h;s}/\mathbf{p}_t\, \mathbf{q}_{h;s}.$$

Annual expenditures for any household h interviewed in quarter s of the vertical sample at constant prices of period t is simply defined by:

$$y_{h;t} = 4\, y_{h;s}\, L(\mathbf{p}_t, \mathbf{p}_s; \mathbf{v}_{h;s}) = 4\, \mathbf{p}_t\, \mathbf{q}_{h;s},\ \text{if } t = \text{winter 1991}$$

$$4\, y_{h;s}/P(\mathbf{p}_t, \mathbf{p}_s; \mathbf{v}_{h;s}) = 4\, \mathbf{p}_t\, \mathbf{q}_{h;s},\ \text{if } t = \text{winter 1987, winter 1981.}$$

In the horizontal case and t = Winter 1991, for each household h we compute a set of four Laspeyres price indices, $L(\mathbf{p}_t, \mathbf{p}_r; \mathbf{v}_{h;r})$, one for each quarter r. Similarly, when t = Winter 1987, Winter 1981, we compute a set of four Paasche indices $P(\mathbf{p}_t, \mathbf{p}_r; \mathbf{v}_{h;r})$. Annual expenditures for any household h of the horizontal sample at constant prices of period t is simply defined by:

$$y_{h;t} = S_r\, y_{h;r}\, L(\mathbf{p}_t, \mathbf{p}_r; \mathbf{v}_{h;r}) = S_r\, \mathbf{p}_t\, \mathbf{q}_{h;r},\ \text{if } t = \text{winter 1991}$$

$$S_r\, y_{h;r}/P(\mathbf{p}_t, \mathbf{p}_r; \mathbf{v}_{h;r}) = S_r\, \mathbf{p}_t\, \mathbf{q}_{h;r},\ \text{if } t = \text{winter 1987, winter}$$

1981.

Finally, as we saw in the first part of this Section, we can compute a set of household specific inflation rates from our three reference periods. For any household h in either the vertical or the horizontal sample, and for any distinct t, t' = Winter 1991, Winter 1987, Winter 1981, the ratios $y_{h;t'}/y_{h;t}$ provide a lower bound for the true inflation rate between period t and t' according to this household preferences.

F. Comparison of the Different Samples

The horizontal sample includes data from 6,284 consumer units participating in CEX Interviews during the January 1990-December 1991 period with a minimum of two interviews (see Table 2). Of these, 5,590 live in urban areas, as defined by the CPI, and 694 live in rural areas. The vertical sample includes 18,986 consumer unit interviews, with 16,857 consumer units living in urban areas and 2,129 living in rural areas.

CEX Diary and Interview Samples. Table 2, columns 1 and 2 include the means and the percentage distributions for selected consume unit characteristics of the CEX Diary and Interview. These are compared to determine if the Diary and Interview samples are similar enough to support our use of Diary reports to impute and allocate expenditures to the Interview sample. In general, we find that the Diary and Interview samples are quite similar. Small differences emerge between the two survey samples for the number of persons in the consumer unit, the race of the reference person, and the number of earners. Consumer units in the Diary are slightly more likely than Interview consumer units to have consumer units with two persons only. The percentage of consumer units with 2 earners in the Diary sample is marginally higher than the percentage of consumer units with 2 earners in the Interview sample.

CEX Samples versus Study Samples. Since we wanted to determine how well our study samples are like the samples from which the expenditure weights are drawn, we compare the characteristics of the CEX samples (columns 1 and 2) with the study horizontal Interview (column 3) and vertical Interview (column 6) samples. We see that the characteristics of all of these samples are quite similar. However, the study samples tend to have reference persons who are slightly older than those in the CEX samples, and tend to have slightly greater percentages of consumer units with 3 or more persons. The CEX samples and the vertical study sample are more alike in terms of regional distribution than is the horizontal sample. In terms of CPI index area, the CEX samples and the study samples have almost identical distributions.

Horizontal versus Vertical Samples. When comparing the horizontal and vertical Interview samples (see columns 3 and 6 in Table 2), we see that consumer unit characteristics are fairly similar with a few notable exceptions. The average age of the reference person tends to be slightly lower in the horizontal sample than in the vertical sample. The horizontal sample is composed of slightly more consumer units with one person and those with three persons, more female reference persons, and a smaller percentage of consumer units with non-black reference persons. Consumer units with one earner are more common in the horizontal sample while those with no earners, with 2 or more earners are more common in the vertical sample. The greatest difference between the horizontal and vertical samples appears to be the regional characteristics "Midwest"; approximately 27 percent of the horizontal sample lives in the Midwest while only about 22 percent of the vertical sample consumer units live in the region. The horizontal sample also includes greater percentages of consumer units living in the South and West, but the percentage difference is quite small. In terms of distribution by CPI index area, the horizontal and vertical samples are again quite similar (see columns 3 and 6 in Table 2).

Urban versus Rural Samples. The percentage distributions of consumer units living in urban only and rural only areas are also presented in Table 2: columns 4 and 5 for the horizontal sample and 7 and 8 for the vertical sample. The characteristics distribution of consumers units in the horizontal and vertical rural subsamples are the same with one exception, as are the horizontal and vertical urban subsamples. The exception is that consumer units of size three are more prevalent in the horizontal urban sample than in the rural horizontal sample. In contrast, in the vertical urban sample they are less prevalent than in the rural vertical sample. The differences between the subsamples appear to be more between consumer units living in urban versus rural areas, and not between horizontal and vertical samples. When comparing the urban and rural samples we find consumer units living in rural areas to have more members in the unit, an older reference person, more persons less than 18 years of age, and more persons greater than 64 years of age. A larger percentage of single person consumer units tend to live in urban areas relative to rural areas. There is a greater percentage of consumer units with male reference persons in rural areas and a greater percentage of units with female reference persons in urban areas. There is a greater percentage of

Table 2. Characteristics of Consumer Units Participating in the CEX in 1990-91

	1	2	3	4	5	6	7	8
	Diary Survey[1]	Interview Survey[2]	Horizontal Interview Sample[3]	Horizontal Urban Only[4]	Horizontal Rural Only[5]	Vertical Interview Sample[6]	Vertical Urban Only	Vertical Rural Only
Number of observations	23,654	41,039	6,284	5,590	694	18,986	16,857	2,129
MEANS OF:								
Family size	2.5	2.5	2.6	2.6	2.7	2.6	2.6	2.8
Age of reference person	46.8	47.2	47.6	47.3	49.6	48.0	47.8	49.9
Persons less than 18	0.7	0.7	0.7	0.7	0.8	0.7	0.7	0.8
Persons over 64	0.3	0.3	0.3	0.3	0.4	0.3	0.3	0.4
PERCENT DISTRIBUTION OF:								
Consumer-unit size								
1	26.9	27.4	26.6	27.4	20.3	25.8	26.6	19.3
2	30.7	29.4	29.2	28.8	32.7	29.6	29.2	32.7
3	16.9	17.0	17.6	17.6	17.4	17.5	17.4	18.2
4	14.7	14.9	15.4	15.2	17.1	15.6	15.4	17.1
5 or more	10.8	11.2	11.2	11.0	12.4	11.5	11.3	12.8
Sex of reference person								
Male	64.6	64.9	64.0	62.4	77.1	64.5	63.0	77.0
Female	35.4	35.1	36.0	37.6	22.9	35.5	37.0	23.0
Race of reference person								
Non-Black	90.1	89.0	89.2	88.3	96.4	89.4	88.6	96.0
Black	9.9	11.0	10.8	11.7	3.6	10.6	11.4	4.0
Number of earners								
0	17.2	19.2	18.8	18.8	19.0	19.0	19.0	19.5
1	35.7	36.3	35.2	35.7	32.0	34.5	34.9	30.9
2	36.0	33.6	34.1	34.0	35.2	34.4	34.2	35.6
3 or more	11.1	10.9	11.9	11.6	16.8	12.2	11.9	14.1
Region								
Northeast	26.2	26.8	21.5	22.3	14.8	21.6	22.6	14.1
Midwest	20.5	21.6	26.9	26.0	34.4	22.1	26.2	34.4
South	30.9	29.9	29.9	29.1	36.7	29.8	28.9	37.2
West	22.5	21.6	21.6	22.6	14.0	21.4	22.3	14.3
Area type								
Large MSA	58.2	57.9	57.5	64.3	2.4	57.8	64.8	2.6
Medium MSA	11.1	10.8	10.9	12.2	0.6	10.9	12.2	0.7
Small MSA	13.0	13.2	13.6	15.1	1.3	13.1	14.6	1.2
Urban non-metro	6.9	7.5	7.6	8.4	0.6	7.6	8.5	0.6
Rural	10.8	10.6	10.5	Na	95.1	10.7	na	95.0
CPI index area								
New York	6.2	6.3	6.0	6.8	0.0	6.2	7.0	0.0
Philadelphia	1.7	1.8	1.7	1.9	0.0	1.7	1.9	0.0
Boston	1.7	1.9	1.9	2.1	0.0	1.8	2.1	0.0
Pittsburgh	1.5	1.7	1.7	1.9	0.0	1.7	1.9	0.0
Buffalo	1.6	1.7	1.7	1.9	0.0	1.8	2.0	0.0
Northeast medium-sized MSA	2.4	2.5	2.6	2.9	0.0	2.6	2.9	0.1
Northeast small-sized MSA	2.0	2.3	2.3	2.6	0.0	2.3	2.6	0.0
Northeast urban non-metro	1.7	1.9	1.9	2.1	0.1	1.9	2.1	0.1
Northeast rural	1.6	1.6	1.6	0.0	14.7	1.6	0.0	13.9
Chicago	2.7	2.6	2.6	2.9	0.0	2.7	3.0	0.0

Table 2. Characteristics of Consumer Units Participating in the CEX in 1990-91 (Cont'd.)

	1	2	3	4	5	6	7	8
	Diary Survey[1]	Interview Survey[2]	Horizontal Interview Sample[3]	Horizontal Urban Only[4]	Horizontal Rural Only[5]	Vertical Interview Sample[6]	Vertical Urban Only	Vertical Rural Only
Detroit	1.8	2.0	2.0	2.2	0.1	2.1	2.3	0.2
St. Louis	1.7	1.7	1.8	2.0	0.0	1.8	2.0	0.0
Cleveland	1.8	1.9	1.9	2.1	0.1	1.8	2.1	0.1
Minneapolis-St. Paul	2.0	1.9	1.9	2.1	0.0	2.0	2.2	0.0
Milwaukee, WI PMSA	1.6	1.7	1.8	2.0	0.0	1.8	2.0	0.0
Cincinnati	1.8	1.9	1.8	2.0	0.3	1.8	2.0	0.2
Kansas City	1.5	1.6	1.7	1.9	0.1	1.7	1.9	0.1
Midwest medium-sized MSA	2.0	2.0	2.0	2.3	0.0	2.0	2.3	0.0
Midwest small-sized MSA	3.6	3.5	3.7	4.1	0.6	3.6	4.0	0.0
Midwest urban non-metro	2.0	2.7	2.2	2.4	0.0	2.1	2.4	0.5
Midwest rural	3.7	3.7	3.7	0.0	33.1	3.7	0.0	33.2
Washington, DC	1.8	1.8	1.8	1.9	0.3	1.8	2.0	0.4
Dallas-Fort Worth	1.9	1.8	2.0	2.2	0.0	1.9	2.2	0.0
Baltimore	1.6	1.5	1.5	1.7	0.1	1.5	1.7	0.1
Houston	1.6	1.6	1.7	1.9	0.0	1.6	1.8	0.0
Atlanta	2.1	1.9	1.8	2.0	0.1	1.8	2.0	0.1
Miami	1.8	1.7	1.7	1.9	0.0	1.7	2.0	0.0
Tampa-St. Petersburg	1.6	1.5	1.6	1.8	0.0	1.6	1.8	0.0
New Orleans, LA MSA	1.4	1.4	1.4	1.5	0.1	1.4	1.5	0.1
South medium-sized MSA	5.9	5.5	5.6	6.2	0.6	5.5	6.1	0.6
South small-sized MSA	5.4	5.4	5.3	5.9	0.6	5.2	5.8	0.5
South urban non-metro	1.6	1.8	1.8	2.0	0.0	1.9	2.1	0.0
South rural	4.1	3.9	3.9	0.0	34.9	4.0	0.0	35.4
Los Angeles	4.2	4.3	4.3	4.9	0.0	4.3	4.9	0.0
San Francisco	2.1	2.0	1.9	2.1	0.1	1.9	2.1	0.1
Seattle	1.7	1.7	1.7	1.9	0.0	1.7	1.9	0.0
San Diego	2.0	1.7	1.7	1.9	0.3	1.6	1.8	0.4
Portland	2.0	1.8	1.8	2.1	0.1	1.8	2.0	0.1
Honolulu	1.5	1.4	1.3	1.4	0.3	1.3	1.4	0.3
Anchorage	1.4	1.4	1.4	1.5	0.1	1.4	1.6	0.1
Denver	1.8	1.6	1.5	1.7	0.0	1.5	1.7	0.0
West medium-sized MSA	0.8	0.8	0.7	0.8	0.0	0.8	0.9	0.0
West small-sized MSA	1.9	2.0	2.2	2.4	0.1	1.9	2.2	0.1
West urban non-metro	1.6	1.6	1.7	1.8	0.4	1.7	1.8	0.5
West rural	1.4	1.4	1.4	0.0	12.4	1.4	0.0	12.5

NOTES

[1] Characteristics are for all consumer units participating in the 1990 and 1991 CEX Diary Survey. Each weekly Diary is treated as an independent interview, and statistics are unweighted.

[2] Characteristics are for all interviewed consumer units in the 1990 and 1991 CEX Interview Survey. Each quarterly interview is treated independently, and statistics are unweighted.

[3] The "horizontal" sample is comprised of all consumer units interviewed in 1990 and 1991, with at least 2 of their 4 interviews occurring in or between Q903 through Q912. Data from each Interview were aggregated into one record per consumer unit.

[4] Urban is defined as the CPI-U urban population: all urban households in metropolitan statistical areas and in urban places of 2,500 inhabitants or more. Excluded are urban farmers, rural, Military, and institutional population.

[5] Rural is defined as the non CPI-U population. This primarily includes households living in rural areas, but also includes urban farmers and the military population.

[6] The "vertical" sample is comprised of all consumer units interviewed in and between Q903 and Q912, as long as the consumer unit had a minimum of 2 interviews in and between Q902 and Q913.

non-black reference person consumer units living in rural than in urban areas. Consumer units living in rural areas are more represented in the Midwest and South than the other two regions.

Expenditure values and budget shares using 1990-91 data are presented in Table 3. As expected, the All Items or X207 mean expenditures are greater than those based on Interview items (X141) only. When comparing the mean expenditures for the total (urban and rural combined) horizontal and vertical samples, they are slightly larger for the vertical (both X141 and X207). Mean expenditures for the vertical sample-urban only are greater than those for the horizontal sample-urban only as well. In contrast, mean expenditures for the horizontal sample-rural only are greater than those for the vertical sample-rural only. We expect this difference between the horizontal and vertical sample means because the horizontal sample has the affect of mitigating outliers. For example, a huge vehicle purchase by a consumer unit will only count once in the horizontal sample estimate of annual expenditures, but it will count four times in the annualization of the vertical sample expenditures. So this finding is intuitive and expected.

Horizontal versus Vertical. When comparing the budget shares for the horizontal and vertical samples, total sample only, we find some differences between the two sets of values. For example, for the vertical sample, the budget shares for food at home, shelter, and fuels and utilities are greater than the budget shares for the comparable horizontal sample. In contrast, the budget shares for housefurnishings and

28

equipment and transportation are greater in the horizontal-total sample, than in the vertical sample.

Vertical versus Horizontal in Urban and Rural Areas. As for the total samples, the vertical-urban only sample has greater budget shares for food at home, and shelter than does the horizontal-urban sample. The horizontal-urban only sample has greater budget shares for transportation and education than does the vertical-urban only sample. When comparing the budget shares of consumer units living in rural areas we find more differences between the horizontal and vertical samples. For example, for the vertical-rural sample, budget shares are greater for food at home, food away from home, shelter, fuels and utilities, and housekeeping supplies and services than they are for the horizontal-rural sample.

Urban versus Rural. When examining the shares for the horizontal and vertical samples (the pattern is the same for these two samples) we find prominent differences between the shares for consumer units in the urban only versus rural only subsamples. Rural consumer units spend a greater share of their consumption expenditures on food at home, housefurnishings and equipment, transportation, health care, entertainment, and other goods and services. Urban consumer units spend a larger share on food away from home, shelter, apparel, personal care products and services, and education.

IV. Results

The means of annualized consumption expenditures and household specific Paasche indexes are presented in Table 4 for the horizontal and vertical samples. Results are further disaggregated by urban and rural. Descriptive statistics for the

Table 3. Budget Shares for Horizontal and Vertical Samples: 1990-91

	HORIZONTAL SAMPLE						VERTICAL SAMPLE					
	Total		Urban Only		Rural only		Total		Urban Only		Rural only	
	Interview ITEMS only[1]	All ITEMS[2]	Interview ITEMS only	All ITEMS	Interview ITEMS only	All ITEMS	Interview ITEMS only	All ITEMS	Interview ITEMS only	All ITEMS	Interview ITEMS only	All ITEMS
MEANS OF:												
CPI Market-basket expenditures	$26,552	$27,251	$27,108	$27,793	$22,071	$22,893	$26762	$27471	$27,396	$28,089	$21,750	$22,579
Budget shares:												
Food at home	14.4	13.9	14.3	13.8	15.3	14.6	14.9	14.3	14.7	14.2	16.4	15.6
Food away from home	6.9	6.6	7.2	7.0	4.2	4.0	6.9	6.7	7.3	7.0	4.3	4.1
Alcoholic beverages	1.0	1.0	1.0	1.0	0.9	0.9	1.0	1.0	1.0	1.0	0.9	0.8
Shelter	28.6	27.8	29.1	28.3	24.1	23.3	29.8	29.0	30.4	29.6	25.2	24.3
Fuels and utilities	8.8	8.5	8.8	8.5	8.9	8.6	9.3	9.0	9.2	9.0	9.5	9.1
Housefurnishings and equipment	3.7	3.7	3.7	3.6	4.1	4.4	3.5	3.5	3.5	3.4	4.0	4.4
Housekeeping supplies and services	1.1	2.9	1.1	2.9	1.1	2.7	1.1	3.0	1.1	3.0	1.2	2.9
Apparel	4.7	4.6	4.8	4.7	4.2	4.0	4.7	4.6	4.8	4.7	4.3	4.1
Transportation	16.4	16.0	16.0	15.7	19.6	18.9	14.4	14.1	14.2	13.8	16.6	16.1
Health care	6.1	6.0	5.7	5.6	9.0	9.2	6.2	6.1	5.8	5.7	9.2	9.3
Entertainment	3.5	3.5	3.5	3.4	3.9	4.3	3.5	3.4	3.4	3.4	3.6	4.0
Personal care products and services	1.0	1.8	1.0	1.9	0.9	1.5	1.1	1.9	1.1	1.9	0.9	1.6
Education	1.7	1.7	1.8	1.8	1.1	1.0	1.5	1.5	1.6	1.6	1.0	1.0
Other goods and services	2.1	2.1	2.0	2.0	2.7	2.6	2.0	2.0	2.0	1.9	2.6	2.6

NOTES

[1] Interview only items include those CPI market basket expenditures reported in the CEX Interview survey. There are 207 item strata in the CPI market basket. Of these, 122 are defined in whole by items reported in the CEX Interview, and another 16 are defined in part. In addition, aggregate estimates for (a) food at home, (b) food away from home, and (b) alcohol at home are available from the Interview, bringing the total number of items covered to 141.

[2] All-items includes expenditure estimates for all 207 CPI market basket item strata. Of these, 122 are derived exclusively from the interview. An additional 16 are comprised of categories reported in the Interview and categories allocated from the Diary. Food at home, food away from home, and alcohol at home expenditure estimates from the Interview were allocated into an additional 68 items using Diary allocation factors.

30

Table 4. Expenditure Values and Price Indexes for Horizontal and Vertical Samples

	HORIZONTAL SAMPLE			VERTICAL SAMPLE		
	Total	Urban	Rural	Total	Urban	Rural
MEANS OF:						
Total annualized expenditures in 1990-91, CEX definition	**$28,354**	$ 28,772	$ 24,982	**$28,572**	$ 29,038	$ 24,884
Annualized CPI-market basket expenditures, all-items	**27,251**	27,793	22,893	**27,471**	28,089	22,579
Market-basket cost at winter 81 prices	**18,436**	18,766	15,772	**18,557**	18,940	15,524
Market-basket cost at winter 87 prices	**23,461**	23,927	19,705	**23,613**	24,147	19,389
Market-basket cost at winter 91 prices	**27,748**	28,303	23,280	**27,932**	28,570	22,886
Annualized CPI-market basket expenditures, Interview only items	**26,552**	27,108	22,071	**26,762**	27,396	21,750
Market-basket cost at winter 81 prices	**18,048**	18,401	15,200	**18,124**	18,526	14,941
Market-basket cost at winter 87 prices	**22,790**	23,267	18,944	**22,886**	23,426	18,611
Market-basket cost at winter 91 prices	**27,007**	27,574	22,441	**27,125**	27,767	22,029
Household Paasche Indexes						
All-items, 81 to 91	**1.5137**	1.5173	1.4848	**1.5192**	1.5232	1.4870
Interview-only items, 81 to 91	**1.5064**	1.5089	1.4861	**1.5124**	1.5153	1.4889
All-items, 87 to 91	**1.1848**	1.1850	1.1839	**1.1876**	1.1878	1.1862
Interview-only items, 87 to 91	**1.1876**	1.1876	1.1874	**1.1907**	1.1908	1.1903

households specific price indexes are presented in Table 5 for the horizontal and vertical samples and for the X141 and X207 commodity space based indexes. Statistical differences in the horizontal and vertical and X141 and X207 commodity space indexes are presented. For illustration purposes, in Table 6 we examine the distributional impact of changes in prices from 1981 to 1991 and from 1987 to 1991 using our household specific indexes for consumer units of different sizes.

A. Consumption Expenditure Values and Household Specific Price Indexes

In Table 4, average consumption expenditures with and without price adjustment are presented along with the average household Paasche price indexes. For the horizontal and vertical total samples, the annualized CPI-market basket

31

expenditures are very similar when based on the all items commodity space. The same pattern emerges for the Interview only items when comparing the horizontal and vertical sample results. In all cases, expenditures for consumer units living in urban areas are higher than those for consumer units living in rural areas. Average expenditures of the vertical urban sample are always higher than those of the horizontal urban sample. In contrast, in all cases, average expenditures of the vertical rural sample are smaller than those of the horizontal rural sample. From this we conclude that using the horizontal or vertical samples produces the same estimate of mean expenditures; however differences are likely to result for different subgroups of the samples.

When comparing the household specific indexes we find greater differences, although within period and commodity space definition, the indexes are quite similar. For the total, urban, and rural sample based indexes, the vertical sample produces indexes which are slightly higher than those for the horizontal sample in all cases. Thus we can conclude, for our study, the vertical sample exhibits greater price inflation than does the horizontal sample. The indexes for consumer units living in urban areas are higher than those for consumer units living in rural areas. This is not surprising since shelter accounts for about 30 percent of the budget for consumer units living in urban areas but only about 25 percent of the budget for consumer units living in rural areas, and shelter prices increased somewhat faster than the prices of other commodities. Shelter prices increased roughly 7 percent more so than did all-items from 1983 to 1991 and the increase in urban areas (A,B, and C sizes) was roughly 3 percent greater than the urban nonmetropolitan areas (D size areas) which were applied to rural households.

B. Descriptive Statistics for the Household Specific Price Indexes

In Table 5 we present basic descriptive statistics for the horizontal and vertical sample based household specific price indexes. Commodity specific food at home indexes are presented to help us understand the impact of the allocation and imputation of Diary information for certain commodities to Interview consumer units consumption expenditures. Note, this process allowed us to move from the X141 commodity space to the X207 commodity space with the Interview as the basic survey upon which our indexes are based.

In Table 5, as noted for Table 4, the household specific indexes are always greater for the vertical sample when compared to those based on the horizontal sample on average. The same is true when we compare the medians. The ranges, standards errors, and coefficients of variation are also larger for the vertical sample based indexes when compared to those for the horizontal sample. Greater variation in the vertical indexes is expected due to the shorter time period upon which the index weights are based.

For both time periods, 1981 to 1991 and 1987 to 1991, the coefficients of variation for the indexes are greater for the Interview only item based indexes compared to the all items indexes. In contrast the coefficients of variation for the Interview only food-at-home indexes are smaller than those based on the Diary imputation for the X207 commodity bundle. We would expect the Diary imputation

33

coefficients of variations to be greater than those for the Interview only based indexes since we have more price variation within the food-at-home index. Why the opposite pattern results for the commodity space defined in terms of all items versus the Interview only items needs further examination. The Diary imputation based food-at-home indexes, when compared to the food-at-home indexes based on the global questions in the Interview only, produce means and medians which are also smaller.

In order to examine whether the household specific indexes are statistically significantly different from each other, indexes for group=0 are compared. This group is selected for the comparison since it is the only group for which the four quarterly (vertical) interviews are entirely contained in the horizontal sample as well. A statistical test for the difference between two means, based on data from non-independent samples, is used. We test whether differences in the indexes are statistically significant when comparing the horizontal and vertical sample based indexes, and the all items versus Interview only items indexes. Our analysis reveals that there is no statistically significant difference between the horizontal and vertical sample based indexes, using the all items or the Interview-only items, when evaluated at the 0.01 level of significance. However, at the 0.05 level, there is a statistically significant difference between the horizontal and vertical sample based indexes for the following: (1) Interview-only, 1981 to 1991; and (2) all items, 1987 to 1991.

C. Application: Distributional Impact of Inflation

Empirical research has long revealed that different groups are not affected in the same manner by the evaluation of relative prices. For example, Deaton and Muellbauer (1991) report that from 1965 to 1971 in Britain, inflation was relatively neutral across the income (defined in terms of expenditures) groups, however from 1971 to 1975 there was a strong "anti-poor" bias to consumer price indexes. Hollister and Palmer (1972) report that in the U.S. during the 1950's and 1960's that inflation was relatively neutral. However, by the 1970's, relative prices moved against the poor (Williamson 1977). A similar pattern emerged for Canada during these time periods (see Ariat 1977). (For early studies on India, see Iyengar (1967) and Mahalanobis (1972); Jorgenson and Slesnick 1983; for other U.K. studies, see Prais (1959), Nicholson (1975), Lesser (1976), and the references quoted in Muellbauer (1974b); for the U.S., see Michael (1970), Hagemann (1982); and for Spain, see Abadia (1986)).

Table 5. Descriptive Statistics for Household Specific Price Indexes

	Minimum	maximum	mean	median	range	Standard error	coefficient of variation
All-items, 81 to 91							
Horizontal	1.0380	2.2980	1.5137	1.5018	1.2600	0.112	7.372
Vertical	0.7492	2.5478	1.5192	1.5089	1.7987	0.125	8.233
Interview-only, 81 to 91*							
Horizontal	1.0274	2.2874	1.5063	1.4962	1.2600	0.113	7.498
Vertical	0.7465	2.5654	1.5124	1.5046	1.8189	0.127	8.401
All-items, 87 to 91*							
Horizontal	0.8546	1.4900	1.1848	1.1815	0.6355	0.047	3.993
Vertical	0.7346	1.5614	1.1876	1.1859	0.8268	0.053	4.494
Interview-only, 87 to 91							
Horizontal	0.8481	1.4844	1.1876	1.1846	0.6363	0.048	4.031
Vertical	0.7315	1.5710	1.1907	1.1897	0.8395	0.054	4.561
Food at home, 81 to 91							
Diary imputation	1.0033	1.7429	1.4340	1.4631	0.7396	0.149	10.418
Interview-only	1.1877	1.5846	1.4570	1.4677	0.3969	0.068	4.673
Food at home, 87 to 91							
Diary imputation	1.0014	1.3330	1.1862	1.2005	0.3316	0.064	5.369
Interview-only	1.1391	1.3745	1.2210	1.2198	0.2355	0.033	2.671

*For group=0 only consumer units, statistically significantly different at the $\alpha = 0.05$ level but not at $\alpha = 0.01$.

For illustration purposes only, we present the all items indexes for the horizontal and vertical samples for winter 1981 (base period winter 1991) and winter 1987 (base period winter 1991) to examine whether our household specific price indexes differ systematically between poorer and richer consumer units (Table 6). For this analysis, consumer units are ranked from lowest to highest using their 1990-91 annualized CPI market basket consumption expenditures (X141 and X207). Three expenditure groups (low, medium, and high) are used to distinguish poorer versus richer consumer units. Results are presented for each of five consumer unit sizes in order avoid selecting an equivalence scale for the comparison. These results are based on unweighted data.

From 1981 to 1991 and from 1987 to 1991, on average, the price indexes are lower for poorer consumer units than they are for consumer units in the medium and upper expenditure groups. We can interpret this result to mean that the indexes are pro-poor. This pattern is shown for consumer units with 3, 4, or 5 persons in the horizontal sample using the 1981 to 1991 index and for consumer units with 1, 3, 4, or 5 persons for the 1987 to 1991 index. For the vertical sample, this same pattern also exists for all but one of the consumer unit size groups. The exception is two person consumer units using the 1981 to 1991 index. Thus, we conclude that between 1981 and 1991 and between 1987 and 1991, relative price changes were pro-poor, and thus that the relative prices of luxuries rose faster than those for necessities.

Table 6. Distributional Impact of Inflation in the U.S. 1981-91: Paasche Household Specific Price Indexes, All Items

Horizontal Sample

Time Period	Consumer Unit Size	Low			Medium			High		
		n	mean	Std	n	mean	std	n	mean	std
1981 to 1991										
	1	557	1.5361	0.12	558	1.5317	0.11	557	1.5320	0.14
	2	612	1.5226	0.10	613	1.5298	0.12	612	1.5197	0.12
	3	368	1.4875	0.10	369	1.5096	0.10	369	1.5077	0.12
	4	322	1.4807	0.08	323	1.4955	0.10	323	1.5086	0.11
	5	233	1.4703	0.08	234	1.4828	0.09	234	1.5019	0.10
1987 to 1991										
	1	557	1.1861	0.04	559	1.1858	0.04	557	1.1856	0.06
	2	612	1.1879	0.04	613	1.1924	0.05	612	1.1850	0.05
	3	368	1.1772	0.04	369	1.1888	0.05	369	1.1809	0.05
	4	322	1.1798	0.04	323	1.1827	0.04	323	1.1855	0.05
	5	233	1.1749	0.03	234	1.1819	0.04	234	1.1830	0.05

Vertical Sample

Time Period	Consumer Unit Size	Low			Medium			High		
		n	Mean	Std	n	mean	Std	n	Mean	std
1981 to 1991										
	1	1632	1.5309	0.13	1633	1.5344	0.12	1633	1.5467	0.16
	2	1875	1.5246	0.11	1876	1.5329	0.12	1876	1.5356	0.14
	3	1108	1.4926	0.10	1109	1.5139	0.11	1108	1.5116	0.14
	4	986	1.4844	0.09	987	1.5056	0.11	986	1.5133	0.13
	5	725	1.4761	0.10	726	1.4952	0.10	726	1.5056	0.13
1987 to 1991										
	1	1632	1.1844	0.05	1633	1.1878	0.05	1633	1.1901	0.07
	2	1875	1.1896	0.04	1876	1.1947	0.05	1876	1.1915	0.06
	3	1108	1.1805	0.04	1109	1.1927	0.05	1108	1.1835	0.06
	4	986	1.1820	0.04	987	1.1886	0.05	986	1.1864	0.06
	5	725	1.1774	0.04	726	1.1878	0.05	726	1.1837	0.06

V. Summary and Conclusions

The primary purpose of this study was to produce household specific price indexes for consumer units living in the U.S. during the early 1990's. Our motivation was to produce indexes for a comparison of real consumption inequality in Spain and the U.S. Because of this comparison we were forced to make certain decisions such that our measures of consumption and prices were comparable for the two countries. To produce the U.S. indexes, we used expenditure data from the CEX for 1990-91 and monthly CPI-U price data from the winter of 1981, the winter of 1987, and 1989-91. The base period was winter 1991.

The household budget survey designs used by Spain and the U.S. differ, so our first decision was to reconcile the differences. We used the Interview component of the U.S. CEX since it is used to collect expenditure data from consumer units over a 12 month period using quarterly Interviews. However, to account for all commodities, we augmented the Interview data with information on the spending patterns of consumer units for certain items using the CEX Diary. By using data from both survey instruments we were best able to match the Spanish design. Second, we assigned to consumer units living in rural areas, as defined by the BLS, relative prices based on the price indexes available from the corresponding urban non-metropolitan areas. The official CPI-U only covers about 84 percent of the total population, while our indexes are designed to cover the total population.

Household specific indexes were produced for what we refer to as two different samples: a horizontal sample and a vertical sample. For the vertical sample, quarterly expenditures are assumed to be independent while for the horizontal sample expenditures are aggregated over the quarters in which the consumer unit participates in the survey. We produced both sets of indexes because we were not sure, *a priori*, which sample would produce the smallest variance.

From our study we conclude that indexes based on expenditures for the horizontal and vertical samples do not differ significantly for the time periods of our study. However, differences in the indexes do result for the urban versus rural samples, with consumer units living in urban areas facing greater changes in relative prices than are faced by consumer units living in rural areas. The all items indexes produced slightly higher index values than did the Interview only item indexes. In our illustration of the distributional impact of relative prices on expenditures, we find relative prices to be pro-poor during the 1980's.

Household specific price indexes could be used to produce indexes for subgroups of the population. Other researchers have examined this issue and have found conflicting results (see references cited earlier supporting the proposition that different groups in the population are likely to have faster or slower growth in their cost of living than recorded by the changes in the CPI-U, and Boskin and Hurd (1985) for a reference not supporting this). However, in the Boskin Report (Boskin et al. 1996), commission members stated that "...work on this subject remains to be done. In particular, the prices actually paid, not just expenditure shares, may differ" (p. 71).

References

Abadia, A. (1986). "Composiciones de demandas, precios relativos y variaciones de capacidad de compra bajo indiciacion de rentas," *Investigaciones Economicas*, pp. 69-81.

Afriat, S. N. (1977). *The Price Index*, Cambridge: Cambridge University Press.

Aizcorbe, Ana M. and Patrick C. Jackman (1993). "The Commodity Substitution Effect in CPI Data, 1982-91." *Monthly Labor Review*. U.S. Department of Labor, Vol. 116, No. 2, December, pp. 25-33.

Amble, Nathan and Ken Stewart (1994). "Experimental Price Index For Elderly Consumers," *Monthly Labor Review*, Vol. 117, No. 5, May, pp. 11-16.

Boskin, Michael J., Ellen R. Dulberger, Robert J. Gordon, Zvi Griliches, and Dale Jorgensen (1996). *Toward a More Accurate Measure of the Cost of Living*, Final Report to the Senate Finance Committee from the Advisory Commission to Study the Consumer Price Index, December 4, 1996. (Also cited as a Committee on Finance of the United States Senate , S. Prt. 104-72, 104th Congress, 2nd Session, William V. Roth, Jr., Chairman, December).

Bureau of Labor Statistics (1997). *BLS Handbook of Methods*, U.S. Department of Labor, Bureau of Labor Statistics, Bulletin 2490. Washington, D. C.: U.S. Government Printing Office, April.

Bureau of Labor Statistics (1995). *Consumer Expenditure Survey, 1992-93*, U.S. Department of Labor, Bureau of Labor Statistics, Bulletin 2462. Washington, D. C.: U.S. Government Printing Office, September.

Consumer Expenditure Survey, 1992-93, Bulletin 2462, Washington, D. C.: U.S. Government Printing Office, September 1995.

Deaton, Angus and John Muellbauer (1991). *Economics and Consumer Behavior*. Cambridge: Cambridge University Press.

Del Rio, Coral and Javier Ruiz-Castillo (1997), *An Inequality Decomposition Method Which Minimizes Equivalence Scales 'Contamination' Problems*, Working Paper 97-42,

Economics Series 19, Departamento de Economia, Universidad Carlos III de Madrid, Calle Madrid, 126, 28903 Getafe, Spain (June).

Del Río, C. and J. Ruiz-Castillo (1996), Ordenaciones de bienestar e inferencia estadística. El caso de las EPF de 1980-81 y 1990-91", in *La desigualdad de recursos. Segundo Simposio sobre la distribución de la renta y la riqueza*, Fundación Argentaria, Colección Igualdad, Madrid. Volumen VI, 9-44.

Del Río, C. and J. Ruiz-Castillo (1997a), "Intermediate Inequality and Welfare. The Case of Spain, 1980-81 to 1990-91", Universidad Carlos III de Madrid, Working Paper 97-38, Economic Series 16.

Del Río, C. and J. Ruiz-Castillo (1997c), *"Poverty Orderings Using Inverse Generalized Lorenz Curves. The Case of Spain, 1980-81 to 1990-91"*,mimeo.

Diewert, W.E. (1987). "Index Numbers: 7. Aggregation Over Consumers," in John Eatwell, Murray Milgate, and Peter Newman (eds.), *The New Palgrave Dictionary of Economics, Vol. 2, E to J*, London: MacMillan Press Limited, pp. 774-775.

Garner, Thesia I. (1993). "Consumer Expenditures and Inequality: An Analysis Based on Decomposition of the Gini Coefficient," *The Review of Economics and Statistics*, Vol. 75, No. 1, February 1993, pp. 134-138.

Garner, Thesia I., David S. Johnson, and Mary F. Kokoski (1996). "An Experimental Consumer Price Index for the Poor," *Monthly Labor Review*, Vol. 119, No. 9, September, pp. 32-42.

Garner, Thesia I., Javier Ruiz-Castillo, Mercedes Sastre Garcis, and Robert Cage (forthcoming 1997). *The Influence of Demographics and Household Specific Price Indexes on Distributions of Expenditures: A Comparison of Spain and the United States,* unpublished manuscript, prepared for the 51st Session of the International Statistical Institute, Istanbul, Turkey, August (to be available from the authors in August).

Hagemann, Robert (1982). "The Variability of Inflation Rates Across Household Types," *Journal of Money, Credit and Banking*, Vol. 14, pp. 494-510.

Higueras, C. and J. Ruiz-Castillo (1992), *Indexes de precios individuales para la economía española con base en 1976 y 1983,* Universidad Carlos III de Madrid, Documento de Trabajo, 92-07.

Hollister, R. G. and J.L. Palmer (1972). "The Impact of Inflation on the Poor," in K. Boulding and M. Pfaff (eds.), *Redistribution to the Rich and the Poor The Grants Economics of Income Distribution.* Belmont, California: Wadsworth.

Iyengar, N.S. (1967). "Study of Differential Price Movements and consumer Behavior: An Application of Fractile Graphical Analysis," *Indian Economic Review*, II, No. 2.

Iyengar, N.S. and N. Bhattacharya (1965), "On the Effect of Differentials in Consumer Price Index on Measures of Inequality," *Sankhya, Series B*, Vol 27, pp. 47-56.

Johnson, David and Stephanie Shipp (forthcoming 1997), "Trends in Inequality Using Consumption-Expenditures: The U.S. from 1960 to 1993," *Review of Income and Wealth.*

Jorgenson, Dale W. And Daniel T. Slesnick (1993), "Individual and Social Cost-of-Living Indexes," *Price Level Measurement*, W.E. Diewert and C. Montmarquette (eds.), Ottawa, Statistics Canada, pp. 241-336.

Kokoski, Mary, (1987), *Consumer Price Indexes by Demographic Group*, Bureau of Labor Statistics Working Paper 167, April.

Kolm, S. C. (1976a), "Unequal Inequality I," *Journal of Economic Theory*, 12: 416-442.

Kolm, S. C. (1976b), "Unequal Inequality II," *Journal of Economic Theory*, 13: 82-111.

Lesser, C.E.V. (1976), "Income, Household Size, and Price Changes 1953-1973," *Oxford Bulletin of Economics and Statistics*, 38: 1-10.

Mahalanobis, P.C. (1972), "Disparities in the Level of Living," in S.L.N. Simha (ed.), *Economic and Social Development*, Vora and Co.

McGregor, Patrick and Vani K. Barooah (1992). "Is Low Spending or Low Income a Better Indicator of Whether or Not a Household is Poor: Some Results From the 1985 Family Expenditure Survey," *Journal of Social Policy*, Vol. 21, No. 1, pp. 53-69.

Michael, Robert T. (1979), "Variations Across Households in the Rate of Inflation," *Journal of Money, Credit, and Banking*, 11: 32-46.

Muellbauer, John (1974a), "Inequality Measures, Prices, and Household Composition," *Review of Economic Studies*, 41: 493-504.

Muellbauer, John (1974b), "Prices and Inequality: the United Kingdom Experience," *Economic Journal*, 84: 32-55.

Nicholson, J.L. (1975), "Whose Cost of Living?" *Journal of the Royal Statistical Society*, Part 4, 138: 540-542.

Prais, S.J. (1959), "Whose Cost of Living?" *Review of Economic Studies*, 26(February): 126-134.

Ruiz-Castillo, J. (1995), *The Anatomy of Money and Real Income Inequality in Spain, 1973-74 to 1980-81*, Journal of Income Distribution, 4, 265-281.

Ruiz-Castillo, J. (1997*, A Simplified Model for Social Welfare Analysis. An Application to Spain, 1973-74 to 1980-81*, Universidad Carlos III de Madrid, Working Paper 97-37, Economic Series 15.

Ruiz-Castillo, J. and M. Sastre (1996), *Indexes de precios individuales con base en 1983 para la Encuesta de Presupuestos Familiares de 1990-91*, Universidad Carlos III de Madrid, mimeo.

Ruiz-Castillo, Javier (1997). *A Simplified Model for Social Welfare Analysis. An Application to Spain, 1973-74 to 1980-81*. Working Paper 97-37, Economics Series 15, Departamento de Economia, Universidad Carlos III de Madrid, Calle Madrid, 126, 28903 Getafe, Spain.

Sastre, M. (1997), *Ensayos sobre la desigualdad y el bienestar de la renta y el gasto en España,* Ph.D. dissertation, Universidad Complutense de Madrid, mimeo Sen, A. (1973), *On Economic Inequality,* Oxford: Claredon Press.

Slesnick, Daniel (1990), "Inflation, Relative Price Variation, and Inequality," *Journal of Econometrics,* 43: 135-151.

Slesnick, Daniel (1993), "Gaining Ground: Poverty in the Postwar United States," *Journal of Poliltical Economy,* Vol. 101, No. 1, pp. 1-38.

Snyder, Elenor M. (1961). "Staff Paper 7: Cost of Living Indexes for Special Classes of Consumers," in *The Price Statistics of the Federal Government: Review, Appraisal, and Recommendations, a Report to the Office of Statistical Standards, Bureau of the Budget,* National Bureau of Economic Research.

Williams, Janet L. (1997) "The Redesign of the CPI Geographic Sample," *CPI Detailed Report Data for March 1997,* U.S. Department of Labor, Bureau of Labor Statistics, Washington, D. C., May.

Williamson, J.G. "Strategic Wage Goods, Prices and Inequality," *American Economic Review,* Vol. 67, pp. 29-41.

Appendix 1: Description of Basic Data

1. Consumer Expenditure Survey (CEX)

The CEX has two components: a Diary or recordkeeping survey completed by participating consumer units for two consecutive one-week periods, and an Interview survey in which the expenditures of consumer units are obtained in five interviews conducted every three months. As noted, data from both are used for this study. A consumer unit is defined as a member of a household related by blood, marriage, adoption, or other legal arrangement; a single person living alone or sharing a household with others but who is financially independent; or two or more persons living together who share responsibility for at least two out of three major types of expenses-food, housing, and other expenses. Students living in university-sponsored housing are also included in the sample as separate consumer units.

Survey participants record dollar amounts for goods and services purchased during the reporting period whether or not the payment is made at the time of purchase. The expenditure amounts include all sales and excise taxes for all items purchased by the consumer unit for itself or for others. Excluded for both surveys are all business-related expenditures and expenditures for which the consumer unit is reimbursed.

The Diary and Interview queries independent samples of consumer units which are representative of the U.S. population. For the Diary, about 5,000 consumer units are sampled each year, yielding about 10,000 diaries a year. The Interview sample is selected on a rotating panel basis, targeted at 5,000 consumer units each quarter. About twenty percent of the sample are interviewed for the first time each quarter while twenty percent are interviewed for the last time. Consumer units are interviewed up to five times, at three-month intervals. Data from the first interview are used to 'bound' expenditures for subsequent interviews and are not used in estimation.

In general the Interview is used to collect data on the types of expenditures which respondents can be expected to recall for a period of three months or longer; these tend to be relatively large expenditures. These include items such as those for real property, automobiles, and major appliances, or expenditures which occur on a regular basis, such as rent, utilities, or insurance premiums. A global estimate for food spending is also collected. In contrast, the Diary is used to collect expenditures on small, frequently purchased items which are normally difficulty for respondents to recall. Items for which expenditures are collected in detail in the Diary include the following: food and beverages (both at home and in eating places), tobacco, housekeeping supplies, nonprescription drugs, and personal care products and services. Expenditures incurred by members of the consumer unit while away from home overnight or longer are not collected in the Diary survey. The Interview survey covers about 95 percent of total expenditures. When Interview data are used in combination with those from the Diary for BLS published tables of expenditures a complete accounting of consumer expenditures is provided (BLS (1995)).

2. Consumer Price Index

The official Consumer Price Index (CPI) in the U.S. is used as a summary measure of the effects of price changes on individual households or consumer units in the population. The CPI is a modified (modified in the sense we use expenditures with prices and implicit quantities) Laspeyres fixed weight index whose weights are the households' mean expenditure shares. This index however does not represent the effect of price changes for each individual household in the population. However, it is often used to adjust incomes and benefit levels for various groups of individuals in the population.

The CPI is a measure of the average change in prices over a fixed market basket of goods and services. The CPI is based on prices of food, clothing, shelter, fuels, transportation fares, charges for doctors' and dentists' services, medicine, and other goods that people buy for day-to-day living. Prices are collected in 85 urban areas (including metropolitan areas and urban parts of nonmetropolitan areas) across the country from about 57,000 housing units and approximately 19,000 retail establishments. All taxes directly associated with the purchase and the use of items are included in the index (see BLS (1997)).

Appendix 2: Item Strata

Interview Only	Interview & Diary	Item Strata	
X141 items	X207 items	Code	Description of Item Strata
Global food at home	D^2	0101	Flour and prepared flour mixes
Global food at home	D	0102	Cereal
Global food at home	D	0103	Rice, pasta, cornmeal
Global food at home	D	0201	White bread
Global food at home	D	0202	Other breads, rolls, biscuits, and muffins
Global food at home	D	0204	Cakes, cupcakes, and cookies
Global food at home	D	0206	Other bakery products
Global food at home	D	0301	Ground beef
Global food at home	D	0302	Chuck roast
Global food at home	D	0303	Round roast
Global food at home	D	0304	Other steak, roast, and other beef
Global food at home	D	0305	Round steak
Global food at home	D	0306	Sirloin steak
Global food at home	D	0401	Bacon
Global food at home	D	0402	Pork chops
Global food at home	D	0403	Ham
Global food at home	D	0404	Other pork, including sausage
Global food at home	D	0501	Other meats
Global food at home	D	0601	Fresh whole chicken
Global food at home	D	0602	Fresh or frozen chicken parts
Global food at home	D	0603	Other poultry
Global food at home	D	0701	Canned fish and seafood
Global food at home	D	0702	Fresh or frozen fish and seafood
Global food at home	D	0801	Eggs
Global food at home	D	0901	Fresh whole milk
Global food at home	D	0902	Other fresh milk and cream
Global food at home	D	1001	Butter and other dairy products
Global food at home	D	1002	Cheese
Global food at home	D	1004	Ice cream and related products
Global food at home	D	1101	Apples
Global food at home	D	1102	Bananas
Global food at home	D	1103	Oranges
Global food at home	D	1104	Other fresh fruits
Global food at home	D	1201	Potatoes
Global food at home	D	1202	Lettuce
Global food at home	D	1203	Tomatoes
Global food at home	D	1204	Other fresh vegetables
Global food at home	D	1301	Fruit juices and frozen fruits
Global food at home	D	1303	Canned and dried fruits
Global food at home	D	1401	Frozen vegetables
Global food at home	D	1402	Canned and other processed vegetables
Global food at home	D	1501	Candy and other sweets
Global food at home	D	1502	Sugar and artificial sweeteners
Global food at home	D	1601	Fats and oils
Global food at home	D	1701	Carbonated drinks
Global food at home	D	1703	Coffee
Global food at home	D	1705	Other noncarbonated drinks
Global food at home	D	1801	Canned and packaged soup

Interview Only X141 items	Interview & Diary X207 items	Item Strata Code	Description of Item Strata
Global food at home	D	1802	Frozen prepared foods
Global food at home	D	1803	Snacks
Global food at home	D	1804	Spices, seasonings, condiments, sauces
Global food at home	D	1806	Other prepared food
Global food away	D	1901	Lunch
Global food away	D	1902	Dinner
Global food away	D	1903	Other meals and snacks
Global food away	D	1909	Unpriced board and catered affairs
Global alcoholic beverages	D	2001	Beer, ale, and alcoholic malt
Global alcoholic beverages	D	2002	Distilled spirits at home
Global alcoholic beverages	D	2003	Wine at home
Global alcoholic beverages	D	2005	Alcoholic beverages away from home
I[1]		2101	Rent of dwelling
I		2102	Lodging while out of town
I		2103	Lodging while at school
I		2201	Owners' equivalent rent
I		2202	Household insurance
I		2301	Property maintenance and repair services
I		2401	Materials, supplies, equipment for home repairs
I		2404	Other property maintenance commodities
I		2501	Fuel oil
I		2502	Other fuels
I		2601	Electricity
I		2602	Utility natural gas service
I		2701	Telephone services, local charges
I		2702	Water and sewerage maintenance
I		2703	Community antenna and cable television
I		2704	Garbage and trash collection
I		2705	Interstate telephone services
I		2706	Intrastate telephone services
I		2801	Linens, curtains, drapes, sewing materials
I		2901	Bedroom furniture
I		2902	Sofas
I		2903	Living room chairs and tables
I		2904	Other furniture
I		3001	Refrigerators and home freezers
I		3002	Laundry equipment
I		3003	Stoves, ovens, portable dishwashers, window air conditioners
I		3101	Television sets
I		3102	Video cassette recorders, disc players, and tapes
I		3103	Audio components, radios, recordings, and other
	Diary only[3]	3109	Unpriced accessories for electronic equipment
I		3201	Floor/window coverings,outdoor/infant/laundry equipment

Interview Only X141 items	Interview & Diary X207 items	Item Strata Code	Description of Item Strata
I		3202	Clocks, lamps, and decorator items
I		3203	Tableware, serving pieces, nonelectric kitchenware
I		3204	Lawn and garden equipment, tools, hardware
I		3205	Small kitchen appliances, sewing machines, portable heating/cooling equip
I		3206	Indoor plants and fresh cut flowers
I		3209	Unpriced household equipment parts, small furnishings
	Diary only	3301	Laundry and cleaning products
	Diary only	3303	Household paper products, including stationery
I		3305	Other household products, lawn and garden supplies
	Diary only	3401	Postage
I		3402	Baby-sitting
I		3403	Domestic service
I		3404	Other household services
I		3406	Appliance and furniture repair
I		3407	Care of invalids, elderly, and convalescents in the home
I		3409	Unpriced rent/repair of household equipment, sound equipment
I		3501	Tenants' insurance
I		3601	Men's suits, coats, sportcoats, jackets
I		3603	Men's furnishings
I		3604	Men's shirts
I		3605	Men's pants and shorts
I		3609	Unpriced uniforms and other clothing
I		3701	Boys' apparel
I		3709	Unpriced boys' uniforms and other clothing
I		3801	Women's coats and jackets
I		3802	Women's dresses
I		3803	Women's separates, sportswear
I		3804	Women's underwear, nightwear, accessories
I		3805	Women's suits
I		3809	Unpriced uniforms and other clothing
I		3901	Girls' apparel
I		3909	Unpriced uniforms and other clothing
I		4001	Men's footwear
I		4002	Boys' and girls' footwear
I		4003	Women's footwear
I		4101	Infants' and toddlers' apparel
I		4109	Unpriced accessories and other clothing
I		4201	Sewing materials, notions, luggage
I		4301	Watches
I		4302	Jewelry
I		4401	Other apparel services
I		4402	Apparel laundry and dry-cleaning, excluding coin operated
I		4501	New cars

Interview Only X141 items	Interview & Diary X207 items	Item Strata Code	Description of Item Strata
I		4502	New trucks
I		4503	New motorcycles
I		4601	Used cars
I		4609	Unpriced other used vehicles
I		4701	Motor fuel
I		4702	Motor oil, coolant, and other fluids
I		4801	Tires
I		4802	Vehicle parts and equipment other than tires
I		4901	Automotive body work
I		4902	Automotive drive-train, front-end repair
I		4903	Automotive maintenance and servicing
I		4904	Automotive power plant repair
I		4909	Unpriced automotive repair service policy
I		5001	Automobile insurance
I		5101	Automobile finance charges
I		5109	Unpriced other vehicle finance charges
I		5201	State and local automobile registration, license, inspection
I		5205	Other automobile-related fees
I		5209	Unpriced docking and landing fees
I		5301	Airline fare
I		5302	Other intercity transportation
I		5303	Intracity transportation
I		5309	Unpriced school bus
I		5401	Prescription drugs and medical supplies
	Diary only	5502	Nonprescription drugs and medical supplies
I		5503	Nonprescription medical equipment and supplies
I		5601	Physicians' services
I		5602	Dental services
I		5603	Eyeglasses and eye care
I		5604	Services by other medical professionals
I		5701	Hospital room, in patient
I		5702	Other in-patient services
I		5703	Hospital out-patient services
I		5709	Unpriced rent or repair of medical equipment
I		5801	Commercial health insurance
I		5802	Blue Cross/Blue Shield
I		5803	Health Maintenance Organizations
I		5804	Other health insurance
I		5901	Newspapers
I		5902	Magazines
	Diary only	5909	Unpriced newsletters
I		6001	Sports vehicles, including bicycles
I		6002	Sports equipment
I		6101	Toys, hobbies, and other entertainment commodities
I		6102	Photographic supplies and equipment
I		6103	Pets and pet products
	Diary only	6109	Unpriced souvenirs, fireworks, optic goods

Interview Only X141 items	Interview & Diary X207 items	Item Strata Code	Description of Item Strata
I		6201	Club membership dues and fees
I		6202	Fees for participant sports
I		6203	Admissions
I		6204	Fees for lessons or instructions
I		6205	Photographers, film processing, pet services
I		6209	Unpriced rental of recreational vehicles
I		6301	Tobacco and smoking supplies
I		6309	Unpriced smoking products and accessories
I		6401	Hair, dental, shaving, miscellaneous personal care products
	Diary only	6403	Cosmetics, bath/nail/make-up preparations and implements
I		6501	Beauty parlor services for females
I		6502	Haircuts and other barber shop services for males
I		6509	Unpriced repair of personal care appliances
I		6601	School books and supplies for college
I		6602	Reference books and elementary and high school books
I		6609	Unpriced miscellaneous school purchases
I		6701	College tuition and fees
I		6702	Elementary and high school tuition and fees
I		6703	Child daycare, nursery school
I		6704	Other tuition and fees
I		6709	Unpriced miscellaneous school items, rentals, and other services
I		6801	Legal fees
I		6802	Banking and accounting expenses
I		6803	Cemetery lots and funeral expenses
	Diary only	6809	Unpriced miscellaneous personal services
I		6901	Information processing equipment

[1] "I" denotes expenditure is from the Interview.

[2] "D" denotes detailed expenditure allocated from the Diary to Interview.

[3] "Diary only" denotes that an expenditure amount is imputed for the Interview from the Diary.

www.ingramcontent.com/pod-product-compliance
Lightning Source LLC
Chambersburg PA
CBHW081616170526
45166CB00009B/2994